Gabriele Altpeter
Homemade German Plätzchen:
And Other Christmas Cookies

About The Author

For several years, Gabriele Altpeter has been running kochfokus.de and kochfokus.com - cooking communities in German and English. There, she passionately presents recipes and cooking advice.

She graduated at the Carolo Wilhelmina University in Braunschweig, her hometown, has been happily married for more than 25 years and is the proud mother of two sons. Amongst cooking and baking, she is also interested in reading and sports and likes running with her Golden Retriever.

Connect With The Author

https://facebook.com/gabi.altpeter
https://twitter.com/kochfokus
https://goodreads.com/galtpeter

https://kochfokus.com

Gabriele Altpeter

Homemade German Plätzchen:
And Other Christmas Cookies

SomePublisher

We strive to provide the best experience to our readers.
Find out more at somepublisher.com/philosophy

This book is available in several versions:
ISBN 978-3-945748-00-8 (Paperback)
ISBN 978-3-945748-01-5 (eBook)

1st edition, published in 2014

Book design and typesetting by Benjamin Altpeter
Photos by Gabriele Altpeter

Typeset in Adobe Garamond Pro, Myriad Pro, and Special Elite

SomePublisher is an imprint of
Gabriele Altpeter, Internet Marketing-Services
Schreinerweg 6
38126 Braunschweig
Germany

somepublisher@gabriele-altpeter.im
somepublisher.com

Table of Contents

Introduction

Dear reader!

The sweet scent of almonds and festive spices lies in the air of my kitchen. This scent floods my heart with warm memories of my childhood and I start dreaming of the days when my mother stood in her kitchen and prepared her amazing different kinds of Christmas cakes and the German Plätzchen (cutout cookies). Can you imagine what happened when she just for a short moment did not pay attention to these delicious sweets? My small hands quickly reached for a Plätzchen or two. I guess my mom knew all too well about her child. Does this raise warm memories of your childhood when you could not wait for Christmas to come?

This is the time we call the most beautiful time of the year. In Germany, traditions such as baking for the advent season, Sundays and, of course, for Christmas are very much appreciated. Decorating your home, singing and baking with the children, visiting Christmas markets and, of course, baking Plätzchen and other Christmas cookies are not only wonderful Christmas activities but also create a cozy atmosphere that helps you forget the nasty rain in November. I personally enjoy attending church and sharing time with the people I love. I want everyone to really feel good and cozy.

Now as an adult, my daily life is filled with working, so preparations for Christmas and Christmas Eve come too soon. Every year, it seems to come sooner than expected.

With this book, I want to invite you to come with me on a journey through a happy and peaceful Pre-Christmas period filled with the magic of Christmas and with lots of beautiful and unforgettable moments.

Our journey starts with some essential remarks on the German way of baking Plätzchen (cutout cookies). Then, I introduce 15 of my favorite German Christmas cookie recipes to you. You will get to know how we Germans prepare a shortcrust pastry. Furthermore, you will get some background information on the *Bethmännchen*, the *Heidesand Cookies*, the *Hildabrötchen*, and on the *Elisenlebkuchen*.

Christmas is the time of spending time with each other. It is thus a good opportunity to surprise your host with homemade Plätzchen as a special way of saying "Thank you for the invitation!", but they are also a perfect present for your beloved ones.

My favorite German Christmas cookies are made the way I learned it from my mother. In other words, I had no professional training on baking but whenever I was unsure why a certain recipe did not work the way I tried to bake it I tried to find out the reasons and over the years I gained a lot of experience.

Enjoy this Special Time, the recipes and baking the German Plätzchen!
Wishing you a joyous and blessed Christmas and a peaceful New Year.

Yours sincerely,
Gabriele Altpeter

A Few Essential Remarks before We Start Baking

I think it goes without saying that we clear our workspace, so that is free of unnecessary things, and we also clean the counter top before we start baking. You should also assemble all the tools that the recipe requires, and set them on your counter top so that they are available when you need them. Anyone who has been in the situation where you need a certain tool which is not available when it is needed knows how frustrating this can be. To prevent errors, it is absolutely necessary to make sure you understand all the directions given in the recipe. Furthermore, make sure you have all the ingredients required in the recipe.

In this section, I would like to introduce some essential baking utensils you need to bake the German Plätzchen. In other words, I do not claim that this is a complete list of all the tools or utensils needed to bake cookies. Instead, I just mention the most important ones.

Baking Utensils to Measure

Fortunately, there are many baking utensils which facilitate the preparation of doughs. But before we start baking, we should make sure to measure the ingredients needed accurately. To do this, we need *teaspoons*, *tablespoons*, a *cup*, and sometimes a *kitchen scale* to measure out dry ingredients. It does not matter if it is not an electronic or digital one. If a kitchen scale is not available, a *measuring cup with visible scale* also permits precise control of quantities. To measure liquid ingredients such as water, juice or milk, it is needed anyway.

Utensils for Cutting

To chop, for example a bar of chocolate, a heavy and sharp kitchen chef's knife is the best tool to use. Furthermore, a mortar and pestle are really useful for grinding larger nuts or almonds into small pieces. But above all, you need different cookie cutters to make the German

Plätzchen. Alternatively, you can use a cookie cutting sheet which has the advantage that you do not have to roll out the dough as often as with single cookie cutters.

Baking Paper Sheets

Baking paper sheets are really useful. They are the easiest way to ensure that the cookies will not stick to the baking tray if you line it with parchment paper before you bake the cookies.

Baking Trays

Although it seems quite clear that everyone is equipped with baking trays, it is worth paying some serious attention to appropriate baking trays. For good reason. If you use a low-quality baking tray, it may bend or change its shape with heat. In this case, the heat is not distributed evenly, and your cookies won't be nearly as good as they could have been.

In general, it is better if you bake just one baking tray of cookies at a time. Avoid placing one baking tray above the other because this can cause uneven baking.

Electric Hand Mixer

An electric hand mixer is used to whisk, knead and stir. With its whisk and kneading hook attachments it is a very useful baking utensil because it helps you to make not only dough but also cream-based mixtures.

Perfection Strips

It is much easier to bake cookies with even dough thickness. An even thickness prevents some of your cookies from baking faster than others. That is why I usually put my dough between perfection strips.

Other useful baking utensils are a cooling rack which is used to cool down a cake or cookies, a flour sifter, bench scrapers are very helpful to cut the dough, bowls in different sizes, spatulas that are used to scrap batters down from the sides and the bottom of a mixing bowl and other whisking and stirring tools such as wire whisks to beat eggs for example.

Last, but not least, you need a good rolling pin to roll out the short-crust pastry.

How to Store the Plätzchen (Cutout Cookies)

Although it is hard to resist delicious and freshly baked cookies, you may have to store the remaining ones for later. Here are some useful tips on how to store your homemade cookies:

- In general, it is necessary to allow the cookies to cool completely before storing them.
- Separate crunchy cookies from soft cookies. Do not store them in one cookie box to keep the crisp cookies from losing their crunch.
- To keep the crispy cookies crunchy, put one or two sugar cubes in your cookie box.
- Store your cookies in cookie boxes or containers with a tight fitting lid.
- It is also absolutely necessary to allow icings to dry completely before storing these cookies.
- Separate different flavors (e.g. do not put cinnamon cookies and aniseed ones into one container).
- If you put cookies with icing, marmalade topping or chocolate coat in layers one on top of the other, put a grease-proof paper between the layers to prevent the cookies from sticking together.

Shortcrust Pastry

As the shortcrust pastry (Mürbeteig in German) requires special treatment, I am going to introduce the main factors you have to pay attention to. The shortcrust pastry is also called 1-2-3-dough in Germany. The numbers 1-2-3 stand for the proportion of the ingredients to each other. It is very good to keep this in mind because with this simple mnemonic rhyme you are always able to make cutout cookies no matter if a special recipe is available or not. Now, all you have to keep in mind is that you need one part sugar (e.g. 50 grams), two parts butter (e.g. 100 grams) and three parts flour (e.g. 150 grams). If you like, you can add an egg and that is all you need for a basic shortcrust pastry.

Furthermore, you should know some essentials of how to treat this dough. One important fact is that the ingredients you work with have to be really cool. That is why the butter is taken straight out of the fridge when you start preparing the dough with it. Even your hands have to be cool if you do not work with an electric mixer or a food processor. Cool ingredients help you prevent a sticky dough. If your dough is sticky do not add flour because this would cause tough baked cookies. Just put it into the fridge for a while.

I prefer to do the entire preparation of the pastry with my hands for two reasons. Firstly, I can avoid over-processing it. Over-processing would mean that the baked cookies were too tough. The second reason is that I can feel the pastry's consistency with my hands whereas a machine cannot.

However, if you do not like the idea of preparing the dough with your hands it is, of course, no problem to use a food processor or an electric mixer.

Another fact to remember is that you should use fine sugar, for example powdered sugar, because this sugar dissolves easier than granulated sugar. Here in Germany, we say: "The finer the sugar, the better the texture of your Plätzchen and the more tender are the baked cutout cookies."

If you knead the pastry with your hands, you should follow this sequence:

1. Cut the cold butter into lumps.
2. Put the sugar in a bowl and add the butter lumps.
3. Use your hands to rub the butter into the powdered sugar or knead it with the electric mixer until the sugar dissolves.
4. Sift the flour on your counter top. Then make a well in the middle using your fingers.
5. Put the butter-sugar mixture into the well.
6. Add the egg. With cold hands, quickly knead the flour from the outside to the inside until the flour is completely worked up. You have to do this really quickly so that your dough does not become greasy. Alternative: Let the processing machine work for a short while.
7. Form the dough into a ball and wrap it in saran wrap.
8. Let it chill in the fridge for 30 to 60 minutes because a dough that is too cold will crack and is difficult to roll.

Bethmännchen

The Bethmännchen have their origins in Frankfurt (Main). The rumor says that a French confectioner worked for the family Bethmann. He created this specialty in 1840. The first Bethmännchen were adorned with four almond halves which represented the four sons, but when one of the sons died, the fourth almond half was removed.

Ingredients for the Dough

1 egg white

a pinch of salt

75 g (3 oz.) powdered sugar

30 g (1 oz.) all-purpose flour

250 g (9 oz.) marzipan paste

Ingredients for the Decoration

30 g (1 oz.) peeled almond halves

1 teaspoon whipping cream

1 egg yolk

Preparation

1.

Line the baking tray with baking paper.

Method

1.

Crack the egg and separate the egg white from the egg yolk.

2.

Put the egg white into a bowl and the egg yolk into a cup or a small bowl.

3.

Add a pinch of salt to the egg white and whisk the egg white up until it is stiff. To whisk the egg white, it is really helpful to use an electric mixer because it is easier to do it this way than doing it by hand.

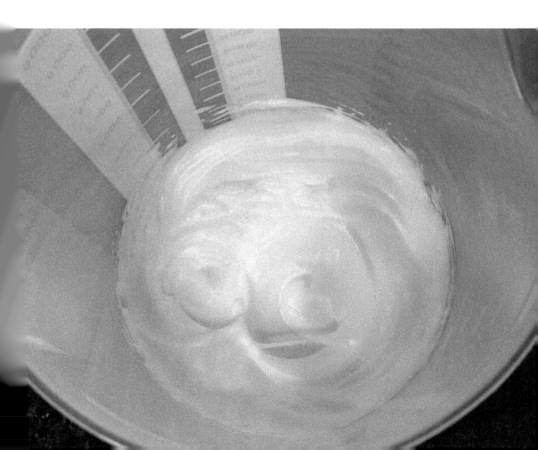

4.

Then finely cut the marzipan paste into small pieces.

5.

Sift the flour and the powdered sugar on your counter top. Then make a well in the middle using your fingers.

6.

Add the egg white and the marzipan.

7.

With your hands, knead the dough until it gets firm, form the dough into a ball, and wrap it in saran wrap.

8.

Let it chill in the fridge for thirty minutes.

9.

In the meantime, cut the almonds into halves.

10.

Then add the whipping cream to the egg yolk and whisk well.

11.

Preheat the oven to 175 degrees Celsius (350 degrees Fahrenheit) upper and lower heat and get the dough out of the fridge.

12.

With wet hands, form the dough into balls and brush them with the mixture of the the whipping cream and the egg yolk.

13.

Adorn the Bethmännchen with three almond halves and place the balls one inch apart on a baking tray lined with parchment paper.

14.

Finally, place the baking tray on the middle rack in the preheated oven and bake for 12 to 15 minutes until they have a nice golden sheen.

15.

Remove the Bethmännchen from the baking tray, place them on a cooling rack, and allow them to cool completely, before serving or storing them.

23

Butterplätzchen
Shortbread Cookies

Ingredients for the Dough

1 middle-sized egg

100 g (4 oz.) powdered sugar

200 g (7 oz.) cold butter

300 g (11 oz.) all-purpose flour (plus additional for the work surface, the rolling pin and the cookie cutters)

Ingredients for the Powdered Sugar Icing

100 g (4 oz.) powdered sugar

3 tablespoons lemon juice

Decoration

You can use sugar sprinkles, chocolate sprinkles, dragées, chocolate beans, nuts or candied fruits to taste.

Preparation

1.

Line the baking tray with baking paper.

Method

1.

Cut the cold butter into lumps.

2.

Put the powdered sugar in a bowl and add the butter lumps.

3.

Use your hands to rub the butter into the powdered sugar or knead it with an electric mixer until the sugar dissolves.

4.

Sift the flour on your counter top. Then make a well in the middle using your fingers.

5.

Put the butter-sugar mixture into the well.

6.

Add the egg. With cold hands, knead the flour quickly from the outside to the inside until the flour is completely worked up. You have to do this really quickly so that your dough does not become greasy. Alternative: Let the processing machine work for a short while.

7.

Form the dough into a ball and wrap it in saran wrap.

8.

Let it chill in the fridge for an hour. Do not leave it in the fridge for too long because a dough that is too cold will crack and be difficult to roll.

9.
Preheat the oven to 170 degrees Celsius (340 degrees Fahrenheit) upper and lower heat.

10.
To prevent the dough from sticking to your work surface, flour your counter top. Lightly flour your rolling pin and dip your cookie cutters in flour, too.

11.
Get the shortcrust pastry out of the fridge and roll the dough to 5 mm thickness (between 1/8 and 1/4 inches).

12.
You may use your favorite cookie cutters and cut the dough into different shapes.

13.
Place the cookies one inch apart on a baking tray lined with parchment paper.

14.

Then place the baking tray on the middle rack in the preheated oven and bake for 10 to 12 minutes until the cutout cookies are set and lightly brown.

15.

Remove the cookies from the baking tray and place them on a cooling rack to let them cool.

Icing

1.

Extract the juice of half a lemon. Here you can use the remaining lemon half from the Zitronensterne (Lemon Stars).

2.

In a medium bowl, combine the powdered sugar and two tablespoons of the lemon juice.

3.

Beat together until the mixture is smooth.

4.

Spread this glaze on the cutout cookies.

5.

If desired, decorate the cookies with sugar sprinkles, chocolate sprinkles, dragées, chocolate beans, nuts or candied fruits.

Cappuccinosand
Cappuccino Heidesand Cookies

Cappuccinosand is another variation of the Heidesand cookies. Do not be surprised that they are tough baked cookies. That is their characteristic. In addition to the original ingredients, they are made of instant cappuccino and unsweetened cocoa.

Ingredients

100 g (4 oz.) butter

150 g (5 oz.) powdered sugar

2 middle-sized eggs

1 tablespoon milk

a pinch of salt

300 g (11 oz.) all-purpose flour

25 g (1 oz.) instant cappuccino

25 g (1 oz.) unsweetened cocoa

Preparation

1.

Line the baking tray with baking paper.

2.

Put the butter into a saucepan and melt it at medium heat until it starts to turn brown. Set aside and let it cool down.

Method

1.

Sift the powdered sugar in a bowl and add the melted brown butter. Whisk the mixture until the sugar dissolves.

2.

Sift the flour on your counter top. Then make a well in the middle.

3.

Put the butter-sugar mixture into the well. Also add the eggs, the salt, the instant cappuccino, the cocoa and the milk.

4.

With cold hands, knead the flour quickly from the outside to the inside until the flour is completely worked up.
Alternative: Let a processing machine work for a short while.

5.

Now shape the dough into rolls of about 2 inches in diameter and wrap them in saran wrap. Let them chill in the fridge for 2 hours.

6.

Preheat the oven to 180 degrees Celsius (360 degrees Fahrenheit) upper and lower heat and get the rolls out of the fridge.

7.

Cut the rolls into equal-sized slices of about 0.2 inches and place these slices one inch apart on a baking tray lined with parchment paper.

8.

Then place the baking tray on the middle rack in the preheated oven. Bake for 20 to 25 minutes until the cookies are set, remove the cookies from the baking tray, place them on a cooling rack and allow them to cool completely, before serving or storing them.

Elisenlebkuchen
Elisen Gingerbread

The Elisenlebkuchen harken back to a German girl called Elisabeth who lived in Nuremberg. When she got seriously ill, her father, a gingerbread baker, created a special Lebkuchen for her. As Elisabeth recovered after a while, these Lebkuchen were called Elisenlebkuchen.

In this recipe, the salt of the hartshorn is used. It is also called smelling salt (for good reason). While baking the Elisenlebkuchen, the scent of ammonia may fill your kitchen. Do not worry about that. The salt of hartshorn is not harmful after baking. However, do not eat the raw dough!

I recommend setting aside enough time for Elisenlebkuchen because the dough has to chill for 24 hours. All in all, it will take two days.

Ingredients for the Dough

4 middle-sized eggs

150 g (5 oz.) Demerara sugar

1 tablespoon vanilla sugar

20 g (1 oz.) all-purpose flour

1/2 teaspoon salt of hartshorn

1 tablespoon gingerbread spice mix (ingredients: cinnamon, anise, cloves, mace, coriander, ginger, and cardamom)

a pinch of salt

1 teaspoon cinnamon

1 tablespoon orange zest

1 tablespoon lemon zest

1 tablespoon unsweetened cocoa

50 g (2 oz.) candied orange peel

50 g (2 oz.) walnuts (chopped)

100 g (4 oz.) hazelnuts (chopped)

100 g (4 oz.) almonds (ground)

wafer papers for baking – round 90 mm papers (if not available 70 mm)

Ingredients for the Powdered Sugar Icing

200 g (7 oz.) powdered sugar

4 tablespoons lemon juice

Decoration

You can use white chocolate Christmas stars, almonds, candied fruits or nuts to taste.

Preparation

1.

Line two baking trays with baking paper.

2.

Place the baking wafers on the baking tray.

Method (First Day)

1.

Finely chop the candied orange peel.

2.

Sift the flour and the unsweetened cocoa in a bowl.

3.

Mix them with the salt of hartshorn.

4.

Then add the pinch of salt, the walnuts, the hazelnuts, the almonds, the candied orange peel, the Demerara sugar, the vanilla sugar, the cinnamon, the gingerbread spice mix, the orange zest, and the lemon zest.

5.

Now add the eggs one after the other and stir well using an electric mixer.

6.

Gently spread equal amounts of the dough onto the wafer papers and leave about 1/4 inch all around.

7.

Let it chill in the cold oven for 24 hours.

Method (Second Day)

1.

Get the Elisenlebkuchen out of the cold oven and preheat the oven to 170 degrees Celsius (340 degrees Fahrenheit) upper and lower heat.

2.

Then place the baking tray on the middle rack in the preheated oven and bake for 15 to 20 minutes.

3.

Remove the Elisenlebkuchen from the baking tray and place them on a cooling rack and allow them to cool completely, before coating them with the icing.

Icing

1.

Extract the juice of a lemon.

2.

In a medium bowl, combine the powdered sugar and two tablespoons of the lemon juice.

3.

Beat together until the mixture is smooth.

4.

Spread this glaze on the Elisenlebkuchen.

5.

If desired, decorate the cookies with almonds, nuts, candied fruits or anything you desire.

Erdnussheidesand-Plätzchen
Heidesand Cookies with Peanuts

The Heideplätzchen are believed to be originated in the Heide which is an area where the Heide (Ericaceae) grows. As the sandy ground on which the Heide grows looks a bit like these cookies, they are called Heidesand. Originally, they were made of very few ingredients. Typically, they are made of melted brown butter which is important for their flavor. Do not be surprised that they are tough baked cookies. That is their characteristic. Today, there is a variety of Heidesand recipes. Here is my favorite one with peanuts:

Ingredients

100 g (4 oz.) butter

150 g (5 oz.) powdered sugar

2 middle-sized eggs

2 tablespoons milk

a pinch of salt

300 g (11 oz.) all-purpose flour

80 g (3 oz.) unsalted peanuts

Preparation

1.

Line the baking tray with baking paper.

2.

Put the peanuts in a mortar and pound them into small pieces with the pestle.

3.

Put the butter in a saucepan and melt it at medium heat until it starts to turn brown. Set aside and let it cool down.

Method

1.

Sift the powdered sugar in a bowl and add the melted brown butter.

2.

Whisk the mixture until the sugar dissolves.

3.

Sift the flour on your counter top and make a well in the middle using your fingers.

4.

Put the butter-sugar mixture into the well.

5.

Add the eggs, the salt, and the milk.

6.

With cold hands, knead the flour quickly from the outside to the inside until the flour is completely worked up.
Alternative: Let a processing machine work for a short while.

7.

Then work in the unsalted peanuts.

8.

Now shape the dough into rolls of about 2 inches in diameter and wrap them in saran wrap.

9.

Let them chill in the fridge for 2 hours.

Erdnussheidesand-Plätzchen

10.

Preheat the oven to 180 degrees Celsius (360 degrees Fahrenheit) upper and lower heat and get the rolls out of the fridge.

11.

Cut the rolls into equal-sized slices of about 0.2 inches and place these slices one inch apart on a baking tray lined with parchment paper.

12.

Then place the baking tray on the middle rack in the preheated oven and bake for 20 to 25 minutes until the Heidesand Cookies are set and lightly brown.

13.

Remove the cookies from the baking tray, place them on a cooling rack and allow them to cool completely, before serving or storing them.

Fruchtige Orangenplätzchen
Fruity Orange Cutout Cookies

Ingredients for the Dough

200 g (7 oz.) cold butter

250 g (9 oz.) all-purpose flour (plus additional for the work surface, the rolling pin and the star cookie cutter)

150 g (5 oz.) powdered sugar

1 middle-sized egg

2 tablespoons honey

a pinch of salt

Ingredient for the Filling

200 g (7 oz.) orange marmalade

Ingredients for the Icing

100 g (4 oz.) powdered sugar

2 tablespoons of orange juice

Fruchtige Orangenplätzchen

Preparation

1.

Line the baking tray with baking paper.

Method

1.

Cut the cold butter into lumps.

2.

Put the powdered sugar in a bowl and add the butter lumps.

3.

Use your hands to rub the butter into the powdered sugar or knead it with an electric mixer until the sugar dissolves.

4.

Sift the flour on your counter top. Then make a well in the middle using your fingers.

5.

Put the butter-sugar mixture into the well.

6.

Add the egg, the salt, and the honey.

7.

With cold hands, knead the flour quickly from the outside to the inside until the flour is completely worked up. You have to do this really quickly so that your dough does not become greasy.
Alternative: Measure all the ingredients into the bowl of a food processing machine and let it work for a short while.

8.

Form the dough into a ball and wrap it in saran wrap.

9.

Let it chill in the fridge for an hour.

10.

Before removing the dough from the fridge, preheat the oven to 170 degrees Celsius (340 degrees Fahrenheit) upper and lower heat, flour your work surface, lightly flour your rolling pin, and dip your cutters in flour.

11.

Get the dough out of the fridge and roll out the dough to about 4 mm (1/8 inch) thickness on the floured surface.

12.

Cut the dough into your desired shapes with 2 inch cookie cutters. I use a round cookie cutter for these cookies. If this is not available, you can use a 2 inch glass.

13.

After that, cut out the center from half of your cookies using a smaller round cookie cutter or another decorative cookie cutter, and place the cookies one inch apart on a baking tray lined with parchment paper. Bake the little pieces you are cutting out separately, because they only need about 6 minutes to be set.

14.

Then place the baking tray on the middle rack in the preheated oven, and bake for 8 to 10 minutes until the cookies are set and lightly brown.

15.

Remove the cookies from the baking tray, place them on a cooling rack, and allow them to cool completely.

Filling

1.

Put the orange marmalade into a bowl and give it a quick stir to soften it up a bit.

2.

Turn the full cookies over so that the bottom is up.

3.

Then spread the bottom-side of the full cookies with orange marmalade and gently top them with the cutout cookies.

Icing

1.

Extract the juice of half an orange.

2.

In a medium bowl, combine the powdered sugar and two tablespoons of orange juice.

3.

Beat together until the mixture is smooth.

4.

Drizzle the cookies with this glaze.

Please note: As the cookies are filled with orange marmalade, they will soften when they are stored.

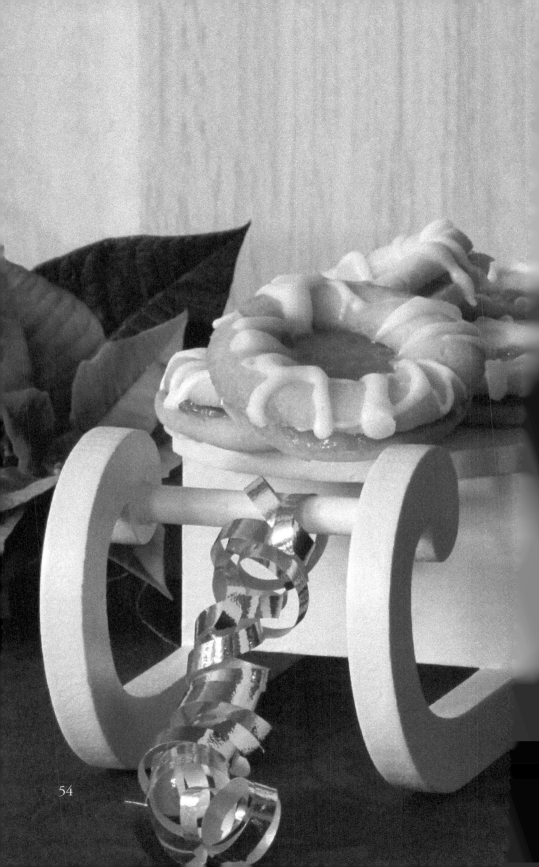

54

Haselnuss-Mandelplätzchen
Cutout Cookies with Hazelnuts and Almonds

Ingredients

250 g (9 oz.) cold butter

150 g (5 oz.) Demerara sugar

1 tablespoon vanilla sugar

a pinch of salt

1 teaspoon baking powder

350 g (12 oz.) all-purpose flour (plus additional for the work surface, rolling pin and cookie cutter)

2 middle-sized eggs

100 g (4 oz.) almonds (ground)

100 g (4 oz.) hazelnuts (chopped)

chocolate baking chips to taste

Ingredients for the Chocolate-Nougat Coating

100 g (4 oz.) dark couverture chocolate

50 g (2 oz.) Nut-Nougat Cuttable Mass

Preparation

1.

Line the baking tray with baking paper.

Method

1.

Cut the cold butter into lumps.

2.

Put the Demerara sugar in a bowl and add the butter lumps.

3.

With your hands, rub the butter into the Demerara sugar or knead it with an electric mixer until the sugar dissolves.

4.

Sift the flour on your counter top. Then make a well in the middle using your fingers.

5.

Put the butter-sugar mixture into the well.

6.

Add the baking powder, the eggs, the salt, the vanilla sugar, the almonds, the hazelnuts, and the chocolate baking chips.

7.

With cold hands, knead the flour quickly from the outside to the inside until the flour is completely worked up. You have to do this really quickly so that your dough does not become greasy.
Alternative: Measure all the ingredients into the bowl of a food processing machine and let it work for a short while.

8.

Form the dough into a ball and wrap it in saran wrap.

9.

Let it chill in the fridge for an hour.

10.

Before removing the dough from the fridge, preheat the oven to 175 degrees Celsius (350 degrees Fahrenheit) upper and lower heat.

11.

To prevent the dough from sticking to your counter top, flour your work surface. Lightly flour your rolling pin and dip your round cutter in flour, too.

12.

Get the dough out of the fridge and roll the dough to 5 mm (1/8 and 1/4 inches) thickness.

13.

Cut the dough into circles and place the cookies one inch apart on a baking tray lined with parchment paper.

14.

Then place the baking tray on the middle rack in the preheated oven and bake for 12 to 15 minutes until the cookies are set and lightly brown.

15.

Remove the Haselnuss-Mandelplätzchen from the baking tray and place them on a cooling rack to let them cool.

Melting the Couverture and the Nut-Nougat Cuttable Mass

1.

Chop the couverture into small pieces.

2.

Cut the Nut-Nougat Cuttable Mass into cubes.

3.

Now add the chopped couverture and the Nut-Nougat Cuttable Mass into a heat-resistant bowl or small pan.

4.

Then fill your boiling pan with water so that it almost comes to the top of the bowl and bring it to a gentle simmer.

5.

Place the heat-resistant bowl onto the boiling pan. Frequently stir your chocolate and the Nut-Nougat Cuttable Mass until it has melted completely.

6.

Remove your heat-resistant bowl from the heat and let the chocolate cool down for a few minutes.

7.

Finally use a teaspoon or fork to drizzle the melted chocolate and nougat over the cookies as desired and cool until it is set.

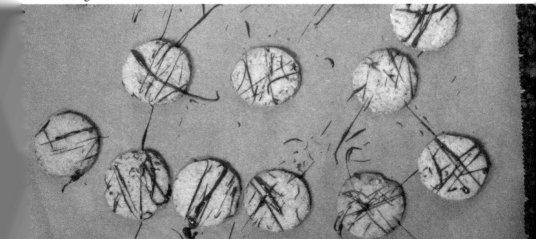

Hildabrötchen

The Hildabrötchen is believed to have originated in the City of Nassau (an der Lahn), where the Grand Duchess Hilda lived. As these cookies were her favorite cookies, they are called Hildabrötchen. Here is the Grand Ducal recipe:

Ingredients for the Dough

130 g (5 oz.) cold butter

300 g (11 oz.) all-purpose flour (plus additional for the work surface, the rolling pin and the star cookie cutter)

125 g (4 oz.) powdered sugar

1 tablespoon vanilla sugar

1 middle-sized egg

a pinch of salt

3 tablespoons powdered sugar

Ingredient for the Filling

250 g (9 oz.) red currant jelly

Preparation

1.

Line the baking tray with baking paper.

Method

1.

Cut the cold butter into lumps.

2.

Sift the flour on your counter top.

3.

Then make a well in the middle using your fingers.

4.

Put the butter, the salt, the powdered sugar, vanilla sugar, and the egg into the well.

5.

With cold hands, knead the flour quickly from the outside to the inside until the flour is completely worked up. You have to do this really quickly so that your dough does not become greasy.

6.

Form the dough into a ball and wrap it in saran wrap.

7.

Let it chill in the fridge for an hour.

8.

Before removing the dough from the fridge, preheat the oven to 170 degrees Celsius (340 degrees Fahrenheit) upper and lower heat, lightly flour your rolling pin, and dip your cutters in flour.

9.

Get the dough out of the fridge, and roll out the dough to about 1/4 inch thickness on a floured surface.

10.

Cut out the dough into the desired shape with 2 inch cookie cutters. I use a Linzer cookie cutter for these cookies. If this is not available, you can use a 2 inch glass.

11.

Then cut out the center from half of your cookies using a 1.5 inch decorative cookie cutter or Linzer cookie cutter, and place the cookies one inch apart on a baking tray lined with parchment paper. Bake the little pieces you are cutting out separately, because they only need about 6 minutes to be set.

12.

Place the baking tray on the middle rack in the preheated oven, and bake for 10 to 15 minutes until the cookies are set and lightly brown.

13.

Remove the cookies from the baking tray, place them on a cooling rack, allow them to cool completely, and dust the cutout cookies with powdered sugar.

Filling

1.

To soften your jelly up put it into a cooking pot and warm it up until it is fluid.
Please note: We warm up the jelly, because we need softened jelly for the filling. Furthermore, the jelly turns back into its original consistency after cooling, and this helps to hold the cookies together.

2.

Turn the full cookies over so that the bottom is up.

3.

Then spread the bottom-side of the full cookies with the warm jelly and gently place the cutout cookie on top, sandwiching the cookies together.

4.

Use a teaspoon to fill the cutout with a little more jelly.

Please note: As the cookies are filled with jelly, they will soften when they are stored.

Honigkuchen-plätzchen
Honey Cake Cutout Cookies

Ingredients

100 g (4 oz.) Demerara Sugar

100 g (4 oz.) honey

50 g (2 oz.) hazelnuts (chopped)

100 g (4 oz.) almonds (ground)

100 g (4 oz.) candied orange peel

100 g (4 oz.) candied lemon peel

1/2 teaspoon cinnamon

a pinch of ground nutmeg

300 g (11 oz.) wheat flour

1 teaspoon baking powder

3 middle-sized eggs

30 g (1 oz.) unsweetened cocoa

Ingredients for the Icing

65g (2 oz.) powdered sugar

1 teaspoon honey

1 tablespoon hot water

Ingredients for the Decoration

peeled almond halves

Preparation

1.

Preheat the oven to 180 degrees Celsius (360 degrees Fahrenheit) upper and lower heat.

2.

Line the baking tray with baking paper.

3.

Finely chop the candied orange peel and the candied lemon peel.

Method

1.

In a large bowl or bowl of a food processor, whisk the wheat flour, the baking powder, the unsweetened cocoa, the cinnamon, and the ground nutmeg together.

2.

Add the eggs, the candied orange peel, the candied lemon peel, the almonds, and the hazelnuts.

Honigkuchenplätzchen

3.

Measure the honey and the Demerara sugar into a cooking pot.

4.

Heat gently until the sugar has melted.

5.

Remove the cooking pot from the heat, let it cool down a bit and add the sugar-honey mixture to the other ingredients.

6.

Using an electric mixer or a food processor, knead well until it gets firm and form the dough into a ball.

7.

Flour your counter top, flour your rolling pin and dip your cookie cutters in flour.
Please note: The dough is really sticky due to the honey. It may thus be useful to flour the surface of the dough lightly, too before the cookies are cut out.

8.

Then roll the dough to 3 mm (about 1/8 inch) thickness.

9.

Cut out into the desired shapes and place the cookies one and a half inches apart on a baking tray lined with parchment paper.

10.

Then place the baking tray on the middle rack in the preheated oven and bake for 10 to 15 minutes until the cookies are set.

11.

Remove the cookies from the baking tray and place them on a cooling rack to let them cool.

Honigkuchenplätzchen

Icing

1.

In a medium bowl, combine the powdered sugar, the honey, and the hot water.

2.

Beat together until the mixture is smooth.

3.

Spread this glaze on the cutout cookies.

4.

Immediately decorate the cookies with peeled almonds.

Marzipan-Aprikosenlebkuchen
Gingerbread with Marzipan and Apricots

In this recipe, I use salt of the hartshorn which is also called smelling salt. This time, your kitchen will not be filled with a sweet scent, but with the scent of ammonia. Do not worry, the salt of hartshorn is not harmful after baking. Do not eat the raw dough however!

The Marzipan-Aprikosenlebkuchen take more time than the other cookies. The dough has to chill for 24 hours. That is why I would recommend setting aside enough time for your Marzipan-Aprikosenlebkuchen. All in all, it takes two days.

Ingredients for the Dough

4 middle-sized eggs

150 g (5 oz.) Demerara sugar

2 tablespoons honey

1 tablespoon vanilla sugar

200 g (7 oz.) all-purpose flour

1 teaspoon salt of hartshorn

1 tablespoon gingerbread spice mix (ingredients: cinnamon, anise, cloves, mace, coriander, ginger, and cardamom)

1 teaspoon lemon zest

50 g (2 oz.) dried apricots

50 g (2 oz.) walnuts (chopped)

50 g (2 oz.) hazelnuts (chopped)

100 g (4 oz.) almonds (ground)

50 g (2 oz.) marzipan paste

wafer papers for baking – round 90 mm papers (if not available 70 mm)

Ingredient for the Chocolate Coating

300 g (11 oz.) dark couverture chocolate

Decoration

You can use white chocolate Christmas stars, almonds, candied fruits or nuts to taste.

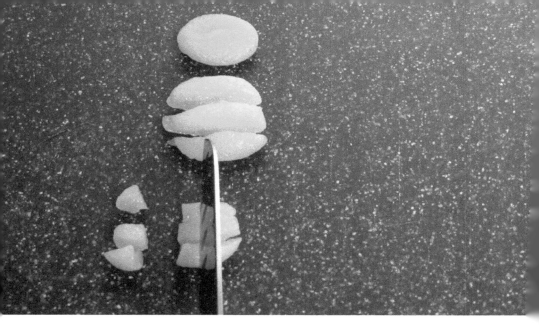

Preparation

1.

Line the baking trays with baking paper.

2.

Place the baking wafers on the baking tray.

Method (First Day)

1.

Cut the apricots and the marzipan finely into cubes.

2.

Put the honey and the Demerara sugar into a cooking pot, bring it to a boil and stir it well.

3.

Then put the eggs, the vanilla sugar, and the lemon zest in a bowl.

4.

Now add the honey-sugar mixture and stir well using an electric mixer.

Marzipan-Aprikosenlebkuchen

5.

Add the almonds, the walnuts, the hazelnuts, the marzipan paste, the apricots, and gingerbread spice mix.

6.

Sift the flour in a second bowl and mix it with the salt of hartshorn.

7.

Then add it to the other ingredients bit by bit and stir well using an electric mixer.

8.

Gently spread equal amounts of the dough onto the wafer papers and leave about 1/4 inch all around.

9.

Let it chill in the cold oven for 24 hours.

Method (Second Day)

1.

Get the Marzipan-Aprikosenlebkuchen out of the cold oven and preheat the oven to 170 degrees Celsius (340 degrees Fahrenheit) upper and lower heat.

2.

Then place the baking tray on the middle rack in the preheated oven and bake for 15 to 20 minutes.

3.

Remove the cookies from the baking tray and place them on a cooling rack and allow them to cool completely, before coating them with the couverture chocolate.

Melting the Couverture

1.

Chop the couverture into small pieces.

2.

Now add two-thirds of it into a heat resistant-bowl or small pan.

3.

Then fill your boiling pan with water so that it almost comes to the top of your heat resistant-bowl and bring it to a gentle simmer.

4.

Place the heat-resistant bowl onto the boiling pan. Frequently stir your chocolate until it has melted completely.

5.

Remove the bowl from the heat and let the chocolate cool down for a short while.

6.

Now add the remaining chopped chocolate to the melted couverture and continue stirring until the remaining couverture has melted too.

7.

Finally, the melted couverture has to be *tempered* that is to say the heat-resistant bowl is placed onto the boiling pan again to warm it up. But make sure not to overheat it. The temperature should not reach more than 32 degrees Celsius (90 degrees Fahrenheit).

Coating and Decoration

1.

Spread the melted couverture on each Marzipan-Aprikosenlebkuchen and decorate it with almonds, nuts or anything you desire.

Marzipanmakronen mit Amaretto
Macaroons with Marzipan and Amaretto

These macaroons with marzipan and amaretto are so-called "Spritz Cookies" that's why you need a pastry bag with an open star tip to squirt the dough onto the wafer papers. *Please note:* The macaroons are made of amaretto. To serve them to children, substitute a tablespoon of juice for the amaretto.

Ingredients for the Dough

2 middle-sized eggs

a pinch of salt

125 g (4 oz.) Marzipan Paste

125 g (4 oz.) butter (softened)

125 g (4 oz.) powdered sugar

1 tablespoon vanilla sugar

250 g (9 oz.) wheat flour

1 tablespoon amaretto

wafer papers for baking – round 40 mm papers

Decoration

You can use candied fruits or hazelnuts to taste and dust the macaroons with powdered sugar.

Preparation

1.

Line the baking tray with baking paper and place the baking wafers on the baking tray.

2.

Remove the butter from the fridge to bring it to room temperature.

3.

Preheat the oven to 180 degrees Celsius (360 degrees Fahrenheit) upper and lower heat.

Method

1.

Crack the eggs and separate the egg whites from the egg yolks.

2.

Put the egg whites into a bowl and the egg yolks into another bowl.

3.

Add a pinch of salt to the egg whites and whisk the egg whites up until they are stiff. To whisk the egg whites, it is really helpful to use an electric mixer because it is easier to do it this way than doing it by hand.

4.

Then cut the marzipan paste and the butter finely into small pieces.

5.

Add the marzipan paste, the vanilla sugar, the butter, the amaretto, and the powdered sugar to the egg yolks.

6.

Using an electric mixer or a food processor, whisk the ingredients up.

7.

Gently fold the wheat flour and the stiff egg whites in.

8.

Fill the dough into the pastry bag, twist the end, and squeeze the dough onto the wafer papers.

Please note: To pipe the macaroons, the end of the pastry back has to be twisted. That is why we only fill half of the pastry bag.

9.

Decorate each macaroon with a candied fruit or a hazelnut.

10.

Place the baking tray on the middle rack in the preheated oven and bake for 12 to 15 minutes until the macaroon cookies are lightly brown.

11.

Remove the macaroons from the baking tray, place them on a cooling rack and allow them to cool completely, before dusting them with the powdered sugar.

Tannenbäume
Christmas Trees

Ingredients

450 g (16 oz.) all-purpose flour (plus additional for the work surface, the rolling pin and the Christmas tree cookie cutter)

2 teaspoons baking powder

100 g (4 oz.) butter (softened)

170 g (6 oz.) white sugar

2 middle-sized eggs

3 tablespoons sour cream (pure and natural)

1 tablespoon lemon zest

Ingredient for the Chocolate Coating

250 g (9 oz.) dark couverture chocolate

Decoration

You can use sugar sprinkles, chocolate sprinkles, small dragées or small chocolate beans to taste.

Preparation

1.

Line the baking tray with baking paper.

2.

Preheat the oven to 175 degrees Celsius (350 degrees Fahrenheit) upper and lower heat.

Method

1.

Cut the softened butter into cubes.

2.

Put the butter cubes into a large bowl and add the sugar.

3.

With an electric mixer, whisk the butter and the sugar until you have a creamy mixture.

4.

Add the eggs, the lemon zest, and the sour cream and stir them into the creamy mixture.

5.

In a second bowl, mix the all-purpose flour and the baking powder.

6.

Sift the flour and baking powder onto your creamy mixture and continue stirring until the ingredients are incorporated.

7.

Knead the dough and form it into a ball.

8.

Flour your rolling pin, and dip your Christmas tree cookie cutter in flour.

9.

On the floured surface, roll out dough to 4 mm (about 1/8 inch) thickness, cut out the Christmas trees and place them one inch apart on a baking tray.

10.

Then place the baking tray on the middle rack in the preheated oven, and bake for 8 to 10 minutes until the cookies are set and lightly brown.

11.

Remove the cookies from the baking tray, place them on a cooling rack and allow them to cool completely, before coating them with the couverture chocolate.

Melting the Couverture

1.

Chop the couverture into small pieces.

2.

Now add two-thirds of it into a heat resistant-bowl or small pan.

3.

Then fill your boiling pan with water so that it almost comes to the top of your heat resistant-bowl and bring it to a gentle simmer.

4.

Place the heat-resistant-bowl onto the boiling pan. Frequently stir your chocolate until it has melted completely.

5.

Remove your heat resistant-bowl from the heat and let the chocolate cool down for a few minutes.

Tannenbäume

6.

Now add the remaining chopped chocolate to the melted couverture and continue stirring until the remaining couverture has melted, too.

7.

Finally, the melted couverture has to be *tempered*, that is to say the heat-resistant bowl is placed onto the boiling pan again to warm it up. But make sure not to overheat it. The temperature should not reach more than 32 degrees Celsius (90 degrees Fahrenheit).

Coating and Decoration

1.

Spread the melted couverture on each Christmas tree and decorate it with sugar sprinkles, chocolate sprinkles, small dragées, small chocolate beans or anything you desire.

Vanillekipferl
Vanilla Crescents

Ingredients for the Dough

300 g (11 oz.) all-purpose flour

2 egg yolks

200 g (7 oz.) cold butter

150 g (5 oz.) almonds (ground)

100 g (4 oz.) white sugar

Ingredients for Dusting the Vanilla Crescents

60 g (2 oz.) powdered sugar

1 tablespoon vanilla sugar

Preparation

1.
Line the baking tray with baking paper.

2.
Whisk the powdered sugar and the vanilla sugar together.

Method

1.
Cut the cold butter into lumps.

2.

Sift the flour on your counter top and make a well in the middle using your fingers.

3.

Put the egg yolks into the well.

4.

Place the butter lumps around the flour.

5.

Now place the sugar and the almonds on top of it.

6.

With cold hands, knead the flour quickly from the outside to the inside until all the ingredients are completely worked up.

7.

Divide the dough into four equal-sized pieces. Form these pieces into rolls of about 20 cm (8 inches) in length and wrap them in saran wrap.

8.

Let the rolls chill in the fridge for 30 minutes.

9.

Before removing the rolls from the fridge, preheat the oven to 175 degrees Celsius (350 degrees Fahrenheit) upper and lower heat.

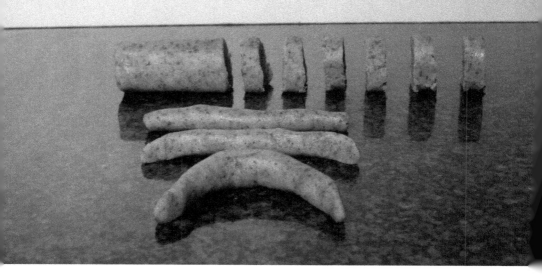

10.

Then get them out of the fridge and cut the rolls into equal-sized slices.

11.

Roll and shape the slices into half moons with slightly pointed ends and then bend the half moons a bit.

12.

Place the crescents one inch apart on a baking tray lined with parchment paper.

13.

Then place the baking tray on the middle rack in the preheated oven and bake for 12 to 15 minutes until the crescent cookies are set and very lightly brown.

14.

Remove the cookies from the baking tray and dust them with the mixture of powdered sugar and vanilla sugar while they are still warm.

Please note: The crescents have to be dusted when they are still warm because the sugar mixture would not stick if they were cold.

Vanillekipferl

Zimtsterne
Cinnamon Stars

Ingredients

3 eggs

300 g (11 oz.) powdered sugar

350 g (12 oz.) almonds (ground, plus additional for the work surface)

1 tablespoon vanilla sugar

2 teaspoons cinnamon

1 tablespoon lemon zest

a pinch of salt

Preparation

1.

Remove the eggs from the fridge to bring them to room temperature.

2.

Sift the powdered sugar into a bowl.

3.

Line the baking tray with baking paper.

4.

Preheat the the oven to 140 degrees Celsius (284 degrees Fahrenheit) upper and lower heat.

Method

1.

Separate the the egg yolks from the egg whites.

2.

Put the egg whites into a large bowl and add a pinch of salt.

3.

Beat the egg whites using an electric mixer with whisk hook attachment until they are stiff.

4.

While beating the egg whites, gradually add the the sifted powdered sugar into the egg whites.

5.

Take away one third of this mixture and set it aside. You will need it later to brush it onto the stars.

6.

Add the remaining ingredients and fold them in gently.

7.

Lightly sprinkle your work surface with ground almonds and roll out the dough to 5 mm (between 1/8 and 1/4 inches) thickness.

8.

Then cut out the stars and place them one inch apart on a baking tray lined with parchment paper.
Please note: It is easier to cut out the stars when the star cookie cutter is dipped into cold water before cutting out each star.

9.

Now take the remaining egg white with powdered sugar and brush it on top of each star.

10.

Place the baking tray on the middle rack in the preheated oven and bake for 15 to 20 minutes.

11.

Remove the cinnamon stars from the baking tray, place them on a cooling rack, and allow them to cool completely.

Please do not throw the egg yolks away. You can use two of them to make the Zitronensterne (Lemon Stars).

Zitronensterne
Lemon Stars

Ingredients for the Dough

200 g (7 oz.) cold butter

400 g (14 oz.) all-purpose flour (plus additional for the work surface, the rolling pin and the star cookie cutter)

120 g (4 oz.) powdered sugar

2 middle-sized eggs

3 tablespoons ground lemon zest

1 tablespoon vanilla sugar

3 – 4 tablespoons lemon juice

a pinch of salt

Ingredients for the Topping

2 egg yolks

100 g (4 oz.) coarse sugar

2 tablespoons whipping cream

Zitronensterne

Preparation

1.

Line the baking tray with baking paper.

Method

1.

Cut the cold butter into lumps.

2.

Put the powdered sugar in a bowl and add the butter lumps.

3.

With your hands, rub the butter into the powdered sugar or knead it with an electric mixer until the sugar dissolves.

4.

Sift the flour on your counter top. Then make a well in the middle using your fingers.

5.

Put the butter-sugar mixture into the well.

6.

Add the eggs, the salt, the ground lemon zest, the lemon juice, and the vanilla sugar.

7.

With cold hands, knead the flour quickly from the outside to the inside until the flour is completely worked up. You have to do this really quickly so that your dough does not become greasy.
Alternative: Measure all the ingredients into the bowl of a food processing machine and let it work for a short while.

8.

Form the dough into a ball and wrap it in saran wrap.

9.

Let it chill in the fridge for an hour.

10.

In the meantime, preheat the oven to 175 degrees Celsius (350 degrees Fahrenheit) upper and lower heat.

11.

To prevent the dough from sticking to your work surface, lightly flour your counter top. Lightly flour your rolling pin and dip your star cutter, too.

12.

Get the dough out of the fridge and roll it to 5 mm thickness (between 1/8 and 1/4 inches).

13.

Cut the dough out into stars, different sizes if you like, and place the cookies one inch apart on a baking tray lined with parchment paper.

14.

In a cup, stir the egg yolks with the whipping cream and coat the stars with this mixture.

15.

Sprinkle the stars with coarse sugar.

16.

Then place the baking tray on the middle rack in the preheated oven and bake for 10 to 12 minutes until the Lemon Star cookies are set and lightly brown.

17.

Remove the stars from the baking tray and place them on a cooling rack to let them cool.

Please do not throw the lemon half away. You can use it to make the powdered sugar icing for the Butterplätzchen (Shortbread Cookies).

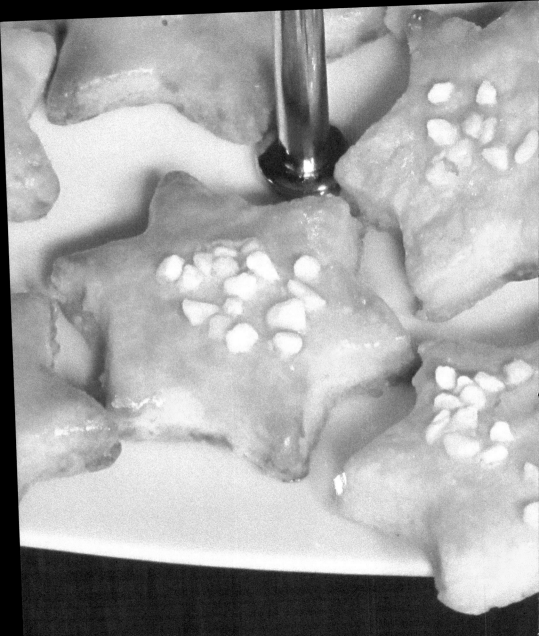

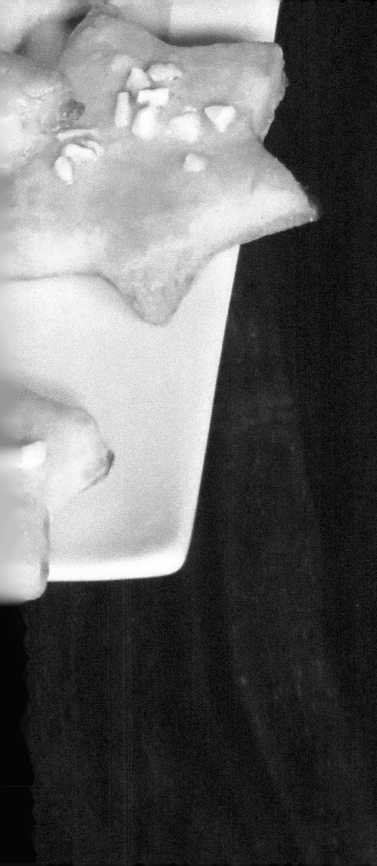